MS Office Quick Tips To Help You Do The Work Of Multiple People

Erik Kopp

www.ekpublications.com

Has This Happened To You?

You have been given the "opportunity" to manage the projects of 4 former coworkers who are suddenly no longer working in your organization, in addition to what you had before. This requires constantly multitasking and shifting focus to keep projects on required timelines and be prepared for team meetings and status updates. Each project has its own archive of key details which you are required to be up on at all times.

Everything seems to be under control, until the VP asks you "what was the original agreement to move forward with this proposal and when was it changed and by whom?" You know you have this information somewhere but now you just cannot pinpoint it in the vast collection of paper and electronic records of various formats and locations. So you spend valuable time desperately searching everywhere you can think of – then you realize that you are now in danger of missing a deliverable on another key project because you have been too tied up on this project, but you still have not located that important memo yet.

Before you give up and totally stress-out, think about how you might be better able to manage your information so that what you need is at your fingertips, ready to whip out in an instant if you are asked for it. Just think - if you could do this how much more valuable you would be to your organization and how much less stress you would feel.

This is entirely possible that you can do this – it just takes a little bit of planning and organization and you will always be able to effectively manage all the information you are responsible for without wasting any time searching for stuff and getting stressed out.

The key to effective information management is to structure your information records such that you consistently know where to find them and how to find them. What follows are real life task management strategies to enable you to maximize your efficiency in managing information; even very large amounts of information.

TABLE OF CONTENTS

The Basics – Task Management to The Rescue

Task management is defined as managing tasks from beginning to end; including planning, tracking and reporting. This is pretty basic stuff, but it often overlooked for seemingly simple tasks or for individual tasks which are part of a larger project. The problem is that when you end up managing 10 or more seemingly simple tasks, you can quickly loose track and get off course; resulting in delays, rework, missed deadlines and lots of stress.

Task management is just that; using tools to keep track of your tasks and key information you need to get your job done effectively. It does not require using MS Project o making Gantt charts. It is just the next level of the simple To-Do list combined with the old "tickler file". These are simple logical tools that can be easily dismissed, but they are very effective and do not require much time to set up.

Give it a try – you have nothing to lose!

Simple Tools To Get and Stay Organized

In order to achieve any kind of meaningful result with a reasonable amount of time, you must have a plan. Just like you need a roadmap to arrive at a destination, the same goes for managing your work. Do not rely on Project Managers or Project Plans or Systems to plan out your work for you. You need to have your own plan to keep you on course.

Your plan must contain all the information you need to reach your objective and it must be kept updated to include current status information because you will be asked for this repeatedly, especially when it is feared that things are falling behind, so you must be prepared to provide this information at all times. It is much better to put this information into your evolving plan document as it happens rather than trying to recreate it later when you are caught off guard and must account for a deliverable which is late. If a deliverable is late because of something beyond your control, it is especially critical that you provide evidence of this ASAP so that the issue gets resolved rather than you being held accountable.

The plan therefore must also include decision-critical information or links to where to find this information in an instant. As organizations are more and more dynamic; people rotate into and out of positions and teams constantly, the rate of change in strategy and direction is much faster than the timelines for many projects. Thus what you are working on right now may no longer be important 3 months from now, in fact it may be a waste of your valuable time to be working on it since the direction of the project has been shifted entirely to some new objective.

Being flexible and changing direction instantly are great traits to have, but the problem is that projects take time to complete and some tasks once set in motion do not instantly change without significant consequences. In the pharmaceutical world, clinical studies take a set amount of time and there are costs that once incurred, cannot be instantly undone if a new marketing VP decided to change course. Likewise capital equipment and real estate transactions cannot be reworked instantly as there are legal and financial consequences.

Where this become a problem for you is when the high-level big-picture people at the top do not realize the scope of impact of their actions and expect everything to fall in line. When it does not, this is when you have to spend a lot of your time fielding questions like:

- Who authorized this?
- Do you have this in writing?
- Why was the contract changed?
- Did the client agree to this?
- What did the original specification contain?
- When did the budget get revised?
- What documentation is in place to support this?
- How did this ever get approved in the first place?

- How many desktop workstations do we currently have deployed at our US facilities? Why haven't these been converted to laptops?
- Who selected this service vendor? For what reason?
- What were these financials based on?
- How quickly can you rework all the spreadsheets to indicate profits in light of the new scope?

You get the idea. If you are the person who worked on this project, you need to be able to answer all of these in a snap.

The key to be able to doing this is before you do any work, set up a plan which will keep track of all this information as it happens so that if you are asked where you are on a project or why something was done, you can refer back to this plan and pull out the information instantly.

I call this plan a tracker because it lays out a roadmap of what I need to do but also keep track of all the loose ends along the way. This is a really valuable skill to master as there are many high level people who are just looking for results and but have little awareness of how many details are required to get to the result. If you can be the person who can effectively manage the details and deliver the desired outcome, you will be very valuable to the organization. The key is to use the details to manage your wok and keep on course but report the high level results to the high level people. If you can keep track of the progress of the details and their relationships to the results, then you are a very valuable asset. If not, things will fall behind and you will need to waste time finding out what went wrong and what got forgotten and what is missing. This is a place you do not want to be.

I make trackers all the time. This helps me manage all sorts of loose ends that I would otherwise soon forget and never get back to without starting over. The tracker should have enough detail to enable you to describe your progress on a project, report on key milestones and to be able to locate any other information you may need in your organization.

The tracker should document tasks are what <u>you</u> can do. These are tasks that you have control over. Big projects beyond your control need to be broken down into manageable tasks that you can manage and control. This is where you have a direct influence over the results of the organization. The starting and ending points of these tasks are where you either need something from someone else or you are delivering something to someone else to enable them to complete their task. In between these points is where you need to the master and keep on course.

The tracker does not need to be very complicated. It should not be so complicated that you spend a lot of time managing it. I use tables in MS Word or Excel to make simple trackers – this is all I need to keep on course.

Start by making a list of all your projects. Then make an outline indicating:

- The name and big objective of the project.

- What steps you need to do to do your part of this project and when these need to be done.

- What you need in order to complete your tasks and who you need this from.

- Running status of where you are and any reasons for delays or not completing the tasks. These are not excuses for not getting something done – these need to be objective business reasons which you can report to your management if you are asked or if you need help. Here is a quick example of good vs. bad reasons for the same issue – need the current financial statement.

  - **BAD**: "Finance has still not provided me the updated report they promised over a week ago." (sounds like complaining and blaming others)

  - **GOOD**: "The forecast is 90% complete but requires the current financial figures to be ready for presentation. As soon as these are available, the completed forecast will be provided." (more objective, stating the facts. There may be a valid reason the financial are not ready to be published yet – this is for someone higher up to find out if you are not given a reason by Finance).

- Supporting information and key decisions. This is where you list what information you have to support the work you are doing and why you are doing it. This includes project charters, memos or emails directing you to do something or justifying why something was done, etc. Be as clear as you can where this information comes from and where to find the original documents. With all the changes in personnel, chances are good that some new director or VP is going to ask you for this because they were not the ones who originally made the decisions and are trying to understand why a certain path was chosen. So hang on to this information and keep a list of it you tracker as this will save you a lot of time later on when you need to pull this out to show it to someone who was not aware of it.

Here is an example of a simple but effective Project Tracker:

Project: Launch Product ABC in Third Quarter.

TASK	THINGS NEEDED / from whom	STATUS / REASONS NOT DONE**	SUPPORTING INFO / KEY DECISIONS
Prepare forecast report for management meeting 01-JUN	1. Figures from 5 key markets. 2. Projected financials from J. Smith. 3. Access to marketing database from IT.	1. Figures received from 3 markets 13-MAY. Remaining not available until August. 2. Financials due 20-MAY. 3. IT ticket opened 100-00045TRBN	1. F. Jones memo 15-MAY: proceed with only 3 markets reporting. C:\ProjABC\Memos\FJ15MAY.pdf
Inform markets of new launch plan by 01-JUL.	1. Approved launch plan from F. Jones. 2. Distribution list from S. Wilson.	1. Available 12-JUN. 2. Received.	1. F Jones contact info: 888-555-1111, FJones@myorganizaton.com

Make sure you have **just one tracker for each project**. This tracker should hold all the key and current information you need to keep on course through the completion of the project. You decide what needs to be in it, but I do not recommend keeping multiple documents around to track projects as these rapidly become out of synch and add to the confusion. Which one do you follow when they are different?

I have often told people "Santa Claus has the best system; he makes one list and checks it twice." Too many projects involve multiple lists and then no one is sure which one is correct so time is wasted figuring this out.

Clearly designate one list as the primary tracker and ensure this one is always up-to date.

If you do this consistently, the small amount of time you spend up front will have you greatly later on when you have moved on and forgotten all these details. The simple question "who authorized this?" can bun through thousands of hours of searching high and low – don't let this happen to you.

How To Find Important Information In An Instant

It's great to save every piece of information electronically, but the downside is that by saving everything you have loads and loads of files, including multiple versions of the same files. Just like with paper records, when the amount of information piles up it becomes very tedious if not impossible to find the one important piece of information you need in the massive clutter you are holding onto.

To avoid this it is very important to be proactive and keep your important information organized so that it is there at your fingertips when you need it so you don't have to waste any valuable time looking and searching for stuff.

This does not take a lot of work to do, but it does take some awareness and planning up front. Here are some **simple tips which will take you less than 10 seconds each to do but could save you hours or more of time looking for vital information**.

1. <u>Decide if a record is important</u> (is it worth saving because you will

need it later? Yes or No?).

If Yes, then proceed to the next step.

If No, then toss it out and eliminate excess clutter.

So how to you decide this?

Every time you are not sure about a piece of information, just ask yourself these simple Yes/No questions:

- Is this information significant (contains information which is vital and hard to find again or it was used to support a key decision, or it is required to be kept by regulation or company policy)?

- Is this information still current and applicable (or was it superseded by more current information and is now outdated)?

- Based on my experience, do I think I will be asked to present or refer back to this information again at a later time?

- If I do not have this file and I do need it later, can I easily recreate it? (i.e. download it from a system or copy it from another location. Retyping it means you cannot easily recreate it).

If you answered Yes to any of these questions, then you need to keep this record. Otherwise, get rid of it now and reduce the clutter which will make finding the really important records more difficult.

If you do need to keep this record, make sure this is done in an organized manner so you can easily find this later on when you urgently need it – please read on.

2. Set up folders to categorize important information.

Now that you have identified a record that really needs to be kept, you need to decide where to keep this. In the electronic world, all records are kept in Folders (what we used to call Directories in the olden days). These can really help keep things organized, but just like paper folders, they can easily become a massive clutter if not set up according to a well thought out plan for maintaining organization and efficiency.

Throwing all important files into a massive "Keep" folder is not a good plan. In a very short time, this folder will be overflowing with lots of files and the time it takes to find the particular one you need will take longer and longer. As newer files come in, it will be difficult to determine if an older version for that file already exists in the "Keep" folder so to be sure this version will most likely also be stored there, as well as others and others... When the "Keep" folder gets too full, you will need to set up a "Keep2" folder which will undergo the same fate so now you will have 2 piles of stuff to dig though to find anything, so this will take even longer. And so on.

Likewise, creating multiple folders all over the place in different locations is not a good idea either because unless there is a plan in place you will not know where to find your information so you will have to search all the folders and you might find the same filename in multiple places with different dates, so now you need to review them all and see which one is the most correct and current. This is another big time waster.

For example, if I was looking for the file below "Basketball Schedule" because the league is asking all coaches to turn these in preparation for the playoff game tomorrow, and I found it in these 2 locations, now I am not sure which one to send to the league. Why are there 2 files? I cannot remember. Did I just save it twice? Or were there changes made to one of them? If so, which is right? Now instead of just grabbing the file and sending it, I need to open each one and review them and compare them....not a good use of my time at all.

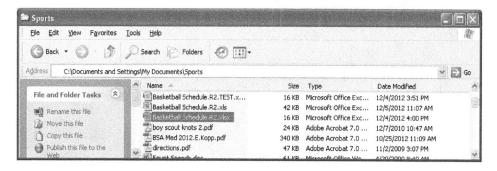

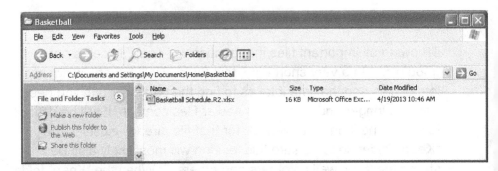

Having said this, saving the file in 2 locations is not a bad idea at all in fact it is a very good idea. The problem is that without a plan, it is not apparent that one is an exact copy of the other. If the file or folder had been labeled as "Backup" or some way to explain its existence this would save a lot of time.

If instead of the screen above, you saw this below – you would be able to get this out much quicker -

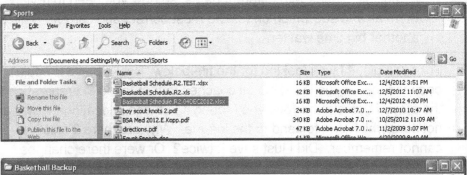

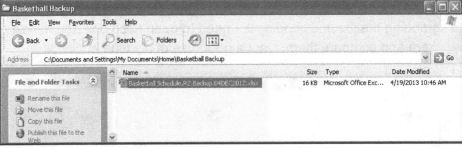

Folders should be set up so that you know what information they contain and it should be very clear which folder contains the primary source of the information.

For example, if you needed to keep track of all your meeting presentations, a good folder structure of doing this is shown below. This is not the only way and may not be the best way for you, but the point is that you need to map or plan this out fist BEFORE you start storing the presentations...

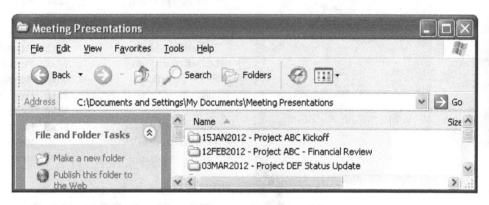

..Or else they may get lost in a folder like this one –

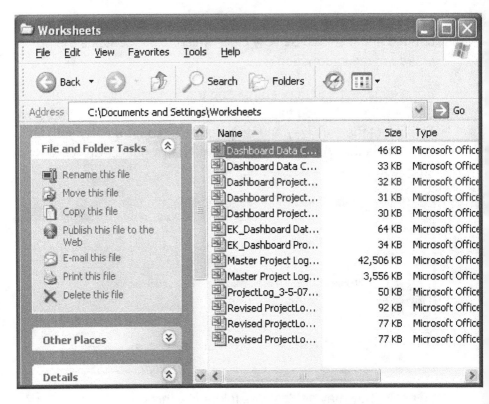

3. <u>Save the record in a format that you will be able to easily and quickly access</u>.

When you save records electronically make sure you can easily find them and you can easily open them. I have come across too many files which require a specific application or version of an application or system which is no longer available, thus the file is not much value any longer and the information may be lost without detailed (and potentially expensive) technical assistance. In either case, the information is no longer at your fingertips and will not be there when you urgently need it.

Plan ahead and make sure you have saved this information in a format most likely to be accessible in the future and from different locations. The best format to use for any kind of documentation is .pdf (Adobe Systems Portable Document Format). This format is readable by any system using a free reader application.

<u>Any</u> document which can be printed can be stored as .pdf.

If the record is on paper, it should be scanned and saved as a .pdf file. Most copiers today are digital so making an electronic file from a copier is very simple. Stand-alone scanners are also really cheap and allow you to do this. For larger volumes of documents and even bound books, there are companies who do this type of conversion work for a living and can help you out for a reasonable cost. It is worth the investment!

If the record can only be opened in a system with limited access (like an online database or website or company software only available on certain workstations) it should be converted to pdf. if you need to save it. One way to do this is to print the record and select the printer as "PDF". This may require Adobe Professional Software or the system may be able to do this already. For example, most of the available Tax Preparation software will do this for you so that you can save you tax returns in a format which can be easily retrieved and printed later if you need it.

This also applies to important emails and other MS Office documents – all should be printed as .pdfs just in case you need this information and cannot open it in the native applications. There are free online PDF converters for MSOffice documents which can help you if you do not have Adobe Professional - just search on "free pdf converter".

4. <u>Name the file so that you know exactly what it is and when it was last revised</u>.

This follows up on the Basketball Schedule example where it is not clear from the file name which one was the correct file we needed. It's great to keep saving and saving and saving different version of the file with different names, but unless there is a logic to the naming which you have planned in ahead, finding the right one when you need it late is going to be a challenging and time consuming task.

A good naming format (and this is just my personal preference) is

"**Project Name.Rev.Date**", or "**ImportanceOfFile.Date**". But use whatever works for you.

Example1: **ProductABCLaunchPlan.R1.19APR2013.xlsx**

Example2: **Product ABC.EUR Forecast.Decision To Delay To Q3.pdf**

You are no longer limited to the old 5.3 file naming format (remember that?) so why limit yourself? Make full use of the technology you have available and make your files names as descriptive as you need them to be to help you find them as soon as you need them.

You do not need to write a story about the file, but make sure name contains the important keywords which will enable you to figure exactly what the file is and also enable a quick and targeted search for the file.

Some quick tips on this –

- Place the most important information about the file at the beginning of the name so that if viewed in a screen which is narrower than the length of the name, you can still figure out what the file is.

- Make sure the name contains key words (text you can use for searches) which uniquely identify the file.

- Make sure the name contains a date and/or revision number so you know which is the most current version of the file. Do not rely on the computer time stamp as this shows when it was last saved, whether you changed it or not.

- If you keep a copy or backup of a file, make sure you include "copy" or "backup" in the file name so you know that it is a backup and not another random version of the file. You can set up MS Office applications to automatically create backups for you every time you save a file. This is very handy.

In MS Word, click the button in the top left –

Then click the Word Options button in the lower right of the window -

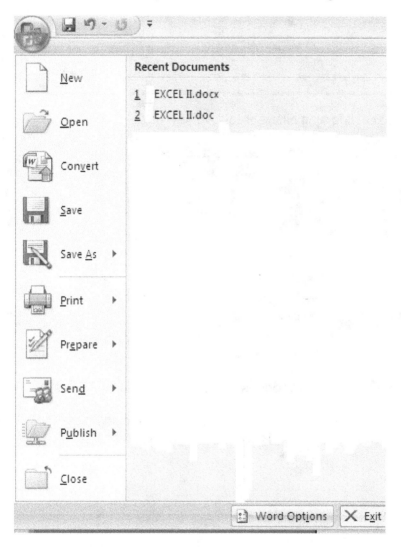

When the Word Options window opens, click "Advanced" in the left hand list and then scroll down until you see "Save" on the right hand side list. Check the box "Always create a backup copy".

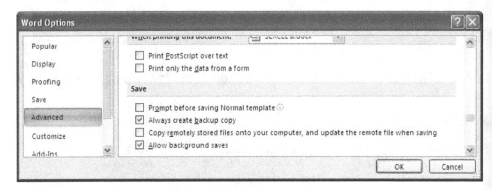

In MS Excel it is a bit different (of course).

In Excel, click the button, then select "Save" –

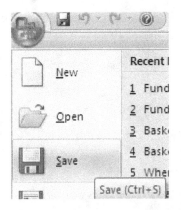

When the Save window opens, click the button called "Tools" –

A list will open. Select "General Options" –

A window will open. Check the box "Always create backup" –

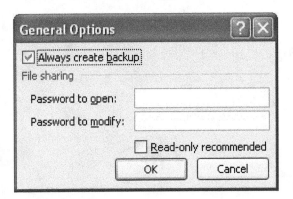

- If you have backup copies, always do your work in the primary file then save it, and then save it as a backup. Always stick to this plan or it is possible to get these confused and accidentally overwrite the new information with the old information.

5. Use special characters to make important files come to the top.

Here is a really quick tip that helps to keep things easy to find. If you use a special character (not letter or number) as the first character in you file name, Windows will sort this so that it comes to the top. For my project files within a folder, I place the character "$" in the front of the one file that is most important to make it easily identifiable so I can go to it immediately without any searching or looking around. If this file is not on the top of the list in the folder view, just click on "Name" until the arrow points up, and the file will come to the top of the list in an instant -

This works for folder names too –

A double character ("$$") will sort higher than a single character.

Just be careful to limit this naming to only the most important file, otherwise everything becomes important and you are back to searching for what you really need again.

Managing All the Loose Ends

Use your electronic calendar to remind you about pending deadlines and include information about what needs to be done, who to contact and where to find information. You have all these technologies available to you so make the best use of them.

If you have a deadline approaching in 3 weeks and you need to complete 4 important steps leading up to this, set up reminders for each of these in your electronic calendar so that you are prompted at least 1 full day before each milestone needs to be complete.

To really make this useful and efficient, include in the calendar reminder specifically what needs to be done. If there any questions to be answered or people to be contacted, be sure to write these in to the calendar reminder. If there is information to be reviewed, attach it to the calendar reminder if you can, o if you cannot then describe where to find it (physical location, URL, folder, server, drive, etc.) in the calendar reminder. The objective is to make your electronic calendar your automated assistant to help you and not just and annoying buzzer to stress you out. Ideally, the calendar reminder pop-up should not only remind you something is coming due, but also provide you with the information and tools you will need to complete this before it's due. The advantage of having it in the calendar is that it is presented to you at the right time when you actually need it. If you tied to keep everything in you awareness all at once now, you would be quickly overwhelmed and lose track 3 weeks from now when this is due.

For example –

If you needed to update an important presentation for management on Project ABC and you have put together as much as could in the prior week (using the strategy of banking you work and planning ahead) but you still need to add in financial information which will not be available until today after 1:30. You know where to find this when it is available and you have an almost completed presentation you spend hours on already. So when you set up your calendar reminder, be sure to include both of these so all you need to do is grab the data and place it in the presentation. You should not have to spend any time at all searching for where the file is and where to find the data. Put these into your calendar when you are actively working on this project and you have this information fresh in your mind. This way you electronic assistant can hand these back to you at the time when you need them again and you can forget about them for a while and work on other things.

Which reminder is more helpful to you? Which one makes you panic more?

This one?

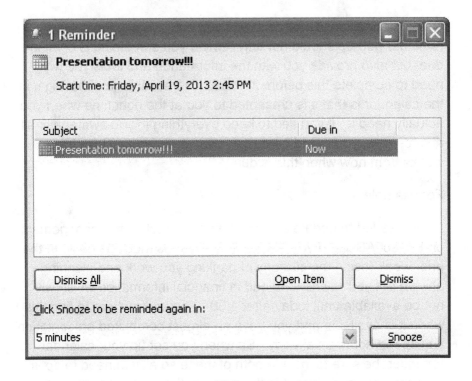

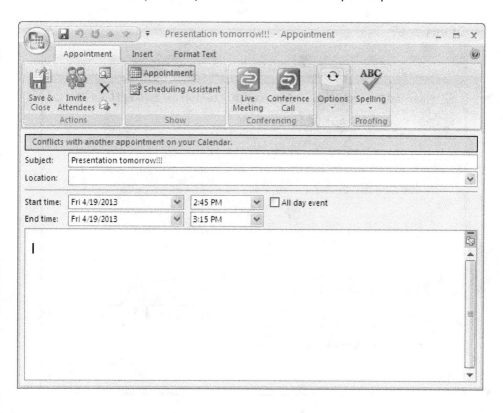

Or this one?

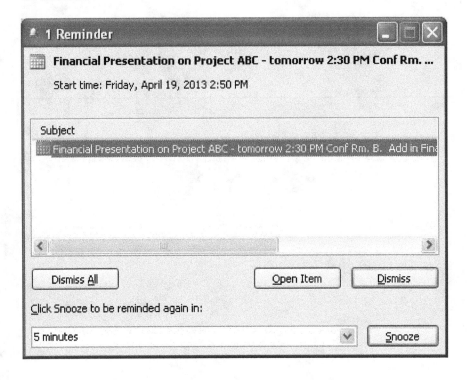

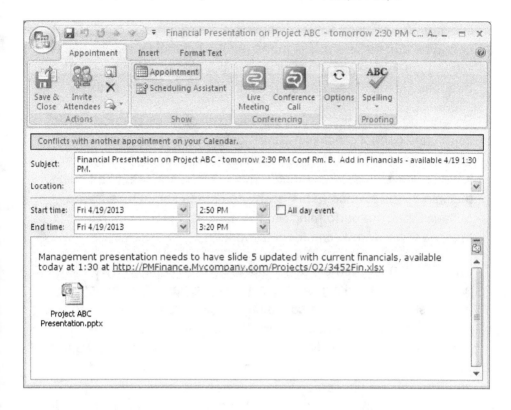

Limit Your Exposure To Distractions

One of the downsides of today's electronically connected world is information overload. We all know this and there are a lot of good sides to being connected; being able to access and share information when you need it and being connected to people all over the world. On the surface this sounds very efficient. But with this ability also come the potential to be constantly interrupted and barraged with many requests and questions and issues and problems and urgent matte which require immediate resolution by you in the minds of the senders.

The problem is that when requests for work and information and attention come in electronically, there is no structure or order to it. The typical email or text at work is "Here is a problem, you fix it and I need it now and just in case people think this is my problem I am copying some other people to show this is now in you court". One or maybe 2 of these a day is manageable, but that is about it. Now with phone, cell, email, IM, and texting the flow of these types of "requests" is multiplied and there is no real order to any of them.

So what do you do first? You cannot do all of these at once. Even computers cannot process multiple tasks at the same time. Although people think they can multitask, the processor only handles one task at a time, but it wok so fast it appears to be doing multiple things at once. This is why computes sometimes freeze – because they are performing another task fist before they can process the one you want them to work on.

The human mind works much the same way. Although we think we are good at multitasking, we are actually just partially completing each task individually and constantly jumping from one to another. Some of us are better at this than others. But facts show that our minds can only effectively focus on one thing at a time if we want to do this well. This is why there are laws about not texting and driving and why you will not see a surgeon answering emails while operating on a patient. If you want to be really good at what you do, you need to be focused on what you are doing and give it your full attention. This is impossible if you are also trying to also focus on providing instant answers to the world's problems on electronic media at the same time.

There have been documented studies which demonstrated that if you are focused on a task, every time you are interrupted, it takes your brain 6 minutes to unfocus from the task at hand and refocus on the new task. Then after you answer whatever it is, it will take another 6 minutes to unfocus from that and get back to where you were – 12 minutes spent on every interruption – that's 1 hour for every 5 interruptions.

Having all these instant communications networks actually makes organization less efficient not more because they are not being used correctly. These have become like automated 2 year olds which need constant attention and instant gratification. These types of impersonal communications presume that you time is free and that anyone who may be uncertain of something and wants to cover themselves will just send out an email asking you to fix something rather than doing more home work on it and figuring out what really should be done. Multiple this by X thousand employees in an organization and you have a lot of wasted time managing email, essentially PR work to preserve your image rather than create value.

Electronic communications email and texts, IMs etc. have great potential of being helpful tools but they are being misused when they are relied upon as a means of assigning work, managing projects or just as an electronic hot potato to shift responsibility and blame on others.

But they can be very hard to ignore

If you had 10 important tasks to complete and mapped out today to get them all done by the end of the day with just enough time to meet all the deadlines, and then you received this email, what would you do?

From: Smith, Joe
Sent: Thursday, April 18, 2013 4:39 PM
To: Kopp, Erik
Cc: Company President, Marketing Director, Finance VP, Erik's Boss, Plant Manager
Subject: Missed opportunity to launch new product line.
Importance: High

Erik,

I think I might have found a mistake in your report which the board is reviewing today, are you sure there are really 0.77 EUROs in a Dollar? Would changing this impact on all the charts?

There are also some more changes we just came up with which could potentially generate 10 Million more in sales, but we need the report now. I tried to catch you last night but you had left to pick up your kids.

Thanks.

Joe

"The value of one's being is measured by the vastness of value one has amassed" **G.Reedy**

\---------------------------------

So here are some strategies to deal with the email/text mania –

- <u>Do not perpetuate the problem</u>.

This is really tempting to sling it right back. But think before you send. Not all emails require immediate responses and if they do you can reply "I will need X time to be able to provide an accurate answer". You've acknowledged their request but you have not taken on the stressful urgency of it.

Try not to "Reply To All" unless you really need to. In the example above, the President and VP may not even have time to read this 1 email out of 1,000 especially if it was sent by someone who is a constant complainer or just wants to be noticed, so don't engage them in their game. Unless you receive a request from one of the VIPs, you do not need to jump and reply to all. If you have done your homework, you should be able to pull the information to support the figures in your presentation and send them to Joe and be done with it and move on to other projects. If he has more information to be added, it is up to him to send this to you which he should have done already instead of wasting everyone's time complaining.

- <u>Communicate Effectively and Efficiently</u>

When you do respond to communications, make sure your communications follow 3 rules – they must be

1. Objective

2. Value-Added

3. Action-Oriented

If you do not follow these 3 rules in all your communication, then you are adding to the muck of confusion. The goals here are to highlight your value to the organization as an expert in what you do and to spend as little time (your time and everyone else's time) as possible on communications while getting the maximum results possible.

So how do this?

First, always be objective; never make unsupported statements which are purely based on your opinion or made in the heat of the moment when your intent is to complain or point the finger of blame at someone. This just perpetuates the negative chain of communications, makes you look bad and wastes everyone's time. If you make a statement indicating that something went wrong because of the actions of another person or group, rather than blaming that group, instead state the current situation and the requirements for moving on to the next step which need something from the person or group in question.

- o **BAD**: "Since Procurement missed the deadline for getting me the current costs by 4 today, there is no way I can get this presentation out on time."

- o **GOOD**: "The presentation is 90% complete, awaiting final costs from Procurement as required by last meeting's action item. As soon as these are received, the presentation will be finalized with the hour."

Second, always provide value added information. When you send out a communication, get to the point and make sure that the communications states clearly what you intend to do, what has been completed thus far and what specific information or deliverables you need and from whom. This provides meaningful information indicating the work you are doing and enables others to help you to achieve you objective and the objectives of the organization. In the example above, the first note just sounds like complaining and does not sound provide any indication of when this will be complete this is a "not my fault" type of complaint which then requires others to figure out what is needed and makes for more follow up notes – waste of time. The second example shows that the work is 90% done and can be ready fairly quickly but states an objective fact that a key piece of information is still needed from another group. This enables others to either help you get this information or make the decision to accept your 90% completed work as this may satisfy their requirements in its present form already. One communication from you and they can figure out all this – very efficient.

Third, always be action oriented. Always keep the result in sight. This means that the objective of all your communications is to get the task finished one time within budget and meeting whatever other requirements there are. Don't bring up problems and obstacles without offering some type of potential solutions. You will not always have all the information nor the authority to have a complete solution, but hold yourself to this standard when communicating a road block –

- Objective statement of the issue and its impacts on the project.

Options:

- Option A: Leave as-is/Do nothing - what impact this will have on the result (costs, timing, quality etc.).

- Option B: Take a specific action - what impact this will have on the result (costs, timing, quality etc.).

- Option C.....

And so on.

You may not have all the answers, but any ideas you can suggest will certainly help out the others in the organization to make better decisions and will go a long way in conveying your value as an expert at what you do.

o BAD: *"The sever just went down due to some loose wires again – just letting you know - I don't know what you want to do about that. It's a big problem. Some people are pretty upset they can't run the reports due today."*

If your job is to manage or maintain the server, never ever ever send out a communication that sounds like this. I've had too many people who worked for me tell me this stuff with no effort on their part to help - they no longer work for me. I could bring in my 5-year old to tell me what's broken and pay them a lot less.

o GOOD: *"The sever just went down due to some loose wires again – we could have XMTService come in and replace the interface board. This will cost $500 for emergency service if needed tonight, or we could move the database to the hot backup server if we contact Jim by 4:30, and then repair the board tomorrow – let me know which makes more sense".*

This second communication is much more action oriented and also provides value added information that enables other to make an effective decision to resolve the problem quickly and reach the desired result; to have the reports run today.

- Avoid unnecessary interruptions

If you take every phone call and answer all emails and texts you will get to spend all your time meeting lots of sales people, trying to solve issues which are above your authority, prove your point a few times, and you'll have at least 30 new magazine subscriptions and have answered 50 surveys. You might even have a few interviews lined up, but you will not get too much important work done because every time the bell rang or the screen flashed or the phone vibrated you jumped and stopped working.

To be really efficient, you must find a way to structure your work so that your brain can process it properly. This means focusing on one primary task at a time until you can get it to a point where you can put it aside without losing that place and having to redo it later.

Emails and texts and phone call are not going to stop so you need to deal with them. My suggestion is to set aside some time each day specifically for the purpose of dealing with emails, texts, etc. Set aside one hour in the morning and one in the afternoon or two in the afternoon, or whatever you need. During this time and <u>only during this time</u>, go though and answer "electronic requests". But outside of this time, work through your planned tasks which you need to finish to meet your deadlines. Stay focused on project work only until email time arrives. This way you can plan out how to accomplish key milestones within project time so that you can focus on email during email time. This may sound clumsy and not efficient, but if you try to do both at once you will end up taking more time to finish both and the results will have more mistakes and be less complete. I know this very well from experience. Try having a conversation with a 2-year old while completing your tax returns and answering a few emails; your 2-year old will be unhappy with you for not paying full attention to them, your emails will be full of typos, and your tax returns will have mistakes you did not notice.

Use Effective Time Management Practices

You may feel like you do not have enough time to get anything done, but you actually have a lot more time than you think. A lot of time passes unnoticed because what you want to do doesn't fit nicely into these time opportunities so whatever it is never even gets started because the ideal time opportunity never shows up. This is a barrier to getting a lot of things done. This is really REALLY important to be able to overcome this barrier.

To overcome this time barrier you need to recognize the time you actually do have and make a plan to ensure it is used wisely to enable you to accomplish whatever it is you think you have no time for.

A VERY important point here: Time Management involves 2 steps:

1. Planning (figuring out what you need to do and when you will do it)

2. Execution (actually doing it)

These are 2 steps which must be completed in this order and must be completed separately. You cannot multitask these together. If you do not have a plan, chances are you will end up spending a lot of time but not get too close to completing the important things you want to get done.

The plan does not need to be very detailed or fancy, but it should describe what needs to be done and when and how it will be done. A rough outline with target dates is fine. Also include sources of information or materials or approvals or whatever you will need to accomplish this. And be sure to define what the deliverable is; what will be the outcome of this work? How do you know you are done?

Making a plan like this does not take much time, but it saves you a lot of time and anxiety later on. A few minutes spend on a good plan will save you months of lost time and extra work.

Next, you need to recognize all the "hidden" time opportunities that can just pass away unnoticed if you do not have a plan to take advantage of them.

In today's ridiculously crazy paced world, time is one of your most valuable assets. You need to use every minute to your advantage. This means that every minute you have available to you should be spent in some productive endeavor.

If you do not constantly hold yourself to this principle, time will slip away without you being aware of how much you could have gotten done during that time. The result will be stress when things are not done or when deadline time comes.

I hear so many people say how they just can't get anything done that they want to get done because they just have no time. I used to be one of these people. I still say this sometimes (to get out of doing things), but I no longer believe it.

The reality is that most people do not have the type of time that they consider to be "available time" or time within their control. In my observation, most people define available time as large blocks of time when they have nothing else to do and they can do whatever they want to do, such as a clear calendar at work or vacation days or weekends when they do not have to work and do not have family responsibilities. These are the only times they consider to be available time, and everything else is beyond their control and unavailable to get anything important done at all.

But actually most people have a lot more available time than they think they just don't count it as available time. This extra time doesn't count for most people because it doesn't fit their definition of available time. It is not a large block of time when they have nothing else to do; it is made up of many small pieces of free time when they may have something else to do.

But this is still available time because you can control how you use it and it can enable you to reach your goals. If you stopped for a minute and added up all the little pieces of free time you really had during the day, the week, the month, the year, you would be amazed at how much there is compared to how little it is being put to good use.

This available time may consist of a couple of minutes here, a couple of minutes there and a couple sometime else, and so on, but added up for a week it may result in several extra hours of time you didn't think you had.

What are examples of this extra available time? Let's name a few:

- Waiting in traffic.
- Standing in line.
- Lunch break.

- Getting up 15 minutes or 30 minutes earlier in the morning, before everyone else is awake.

- Sitting in meetings or in conference calls that contain no action items or information of interest to you.

- Taking your son or daughter to a sports activity.

- Waiting for the dentist.

- Business trips (sitting in planes, waiting in airports, being in hotels, eating meals alone).

- Waiting for the computer to refresh the screen or a page to open or file to download.

- Free time to think and plan while doing manual chores (laundry, dishes, yard work).

This is the next step to using your time wisely; figure out how much time you really have. Go through this exercise and you will be amazed to find you really do have more free time than you think. You just need to change your definition of "available time".

Now that you know how much time you have, the next step is to figure out how to use it effectively. The way to do this is to prioritize your goals, figure out what tasks need to be completed to meet these goals, and then match these tasks to fit into the available time slots. Make sure you include leisure activities, fun and taking care of yourself in your important goals.

Planning is very important to be successful at making the best use of all your free time. You need to be able to break down big objectives into tasks that will fit into the time slots you have. The key is to be creative and flexible. If you can master this skill, you will be amazed at how much more you can accomplish.

For example, if your goal is to landscape your yard, you will not be able to do this while you are in traffic or while you are in a meeting. But if you can break it down to tasks which you can do during these times, you will find that you are much farther along in reaching your goal after a short time, than if you just put it off because you "just don't have the time".

Instead of complaining about not having the time, you could break down the landscaping project into:

1) Doing some research (reading books on landscaping and books on trees).

2) Making phone calls to nurseries and landscapers about availability of materials.

3) Deciding where to plant things.

4) Sketching out a design.

5) Looking through catalogs.

6) Writing out orders.

7) Planning, breaking down the project into the small tasks listed above and coming up with a project plan.

All of these tasks can be fit into small blocks of time. It is possible to sketch out a drawing during a boring meeting, it is possible to look at catalogs when you are waiting for the dentist or on the bus, it is possible to place orders for materials during lunch break. It just takes planning and coordination to figure out what to do and when it can be done.

The result will be that when you get to the point where you have to take a day off to do the actual work of preparing the ground and planting, you will find that a lot of the preliminary work is already done and you are ready to start. So now you can use your large block of free time wisely to do what can only be done during that large block of time, instead of wasting it on a lot of small tasks which you could have accomplished without taking a day off.

Don't fall into the "all-or-nothing" trap that I used to fall into; where unless I had a large block of time (large enough to do the whole thing start-to-finish) then I felt that I just didn't have enough time, and I didn't even start to do anything at all!

This will never get you anywhere you want to go. Break things down and make them fit into the small blocks of time that you do have, and you DO have them.

In the case of work projects, an effective plan is to think ahead and bank completed work. This means that you may not be able to complete the financial reporting statement today, but you realize that you have 20 minutes in which you can download 50 of the 75 spreadsheets you will need – so don't waste this time, download as much as you can. This will save you 20 minutes next week when you are struggling to meet the deadline, and minutes count. If you can set up the presentation while the files are downloading – even better! If you can follow up with key individual on info you need by sending them reminder emails or calling them while the files are downloading and you are tinkering with the presentation – Now You Are The Master Of Your Time!!

Try this technique with all your important tasks; work projects and non-work projects. See how much you can break something down to small pieces that can be fit into your little bits of free time. You will be amazed at how much you can really get done. And you will stop believing that "I just don't have enough time".

Use Automated Tools To Help You Find What You Need

The Windows search tool is a must-use automated assistant which will save your hours and hours of time and aggravation. If you set up your folders and files according to the plan described above, this tool is the icing on the cake which will allow you to effortlessly an instantly pull out key information at the touch of a few buttons.

It is very simple to use so here we go.

First right-click on the folder or drive you want to search in. you should know which folder to look in if the files were organized properly, but if not pick the drive that contains the folder.

Select "Search" -

When Windows Search opens, click on the link "Click here to use Search Companion" – the link next to the little doggie shown below -

When the search companion window opens, enter in as much of the file name as you can on the first line as shown below (this is where your keywords for naming files really pays off) -

Then click "Search" and the results will populate the screen -

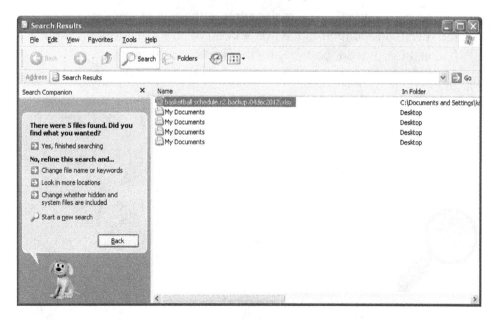

Another option is to search within the files. To do this, type in a word, text string or numbers contained in the file(s) you are looking for on the second line.

Then click "Search". You may get more than what you are looking for. I would recommend the first search option, but if that does not find what you need, certainly try the second afterwards -

How To Create Your Own Backups Of Important Folders and Drives.

Have you ever lost a really important file? You've spent weeks or even months working on a super important file that is due today. Because it is so important, you have saved it on the "share folder" or the "network drive" because this is much more secure than your local hard drive and it is backed up by IT right? But then when the big date arrives, you cannot find the file. Due to a power failure (or network error, or service interruption....you fill in the details_____), the file is not accessible or it is just not there at all.

So you call the Help Desk to tell them you urgently need this file restored from backup. "No problem" they tell you, "we will open a ticket and assign it to the server guys". "How long will this take?" you ask. "We can't day until we hear back from them" is the answer (translation: you're dealing with outsourced people half-way around the world who manage over 10,000 servers and depending on what your company paid for they may not even have a backup since 6 months ago, if they still have it at all.) So now you anxiously wait................

If something like this is really important (it has a significant value in terms of how much wok and/or time it would take to recreate it) then it is a very wise practice to keep current backup copies.

The first thing you need to do is to identify where you are going to store your backup. Most companies do not allow you to store company information (basically all computer files you create while working for the company) on external "cloud" drives, and placing them on your hard disk is risky if it fails and you might not have the space. The best place to keep this type of important information that you cannot afford to lose is on portable mass storage devices (such as external hard drives or USB sticks) which you can keep locked up in a secure area where you will be able to access them if needed, even from another computer.

Once you have a place to store your information, it is very important to keep it up to date on a REGULAR basis. This can be either time based (every week, every other day, every day...) or you can do this every time you update the information; save it in the primary location and then update your back up by copying the file over to the backup media.

Doing this on a regular basis can be very time consuming if you use the basic Windows Copy and Paste commands such as –

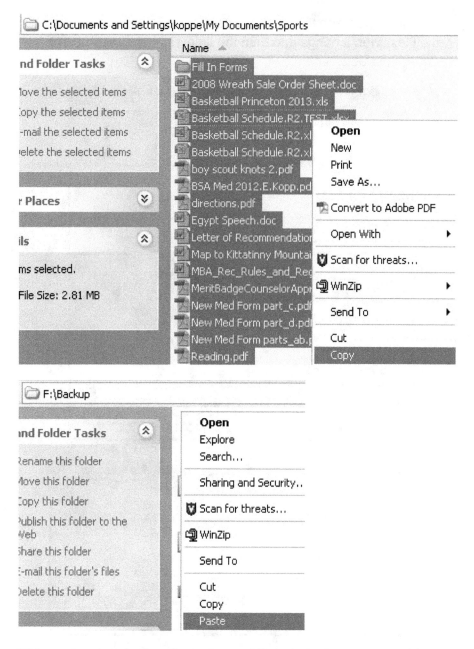

This works okay for small numbers of files, but when you need to copy folders and drives, this can be very time consuming and tedious for 2 reasons –

You get the screen that tells you it will take 35 minutes to copy all the files, then it hangs and then the time estimate goes up and up rather than down –

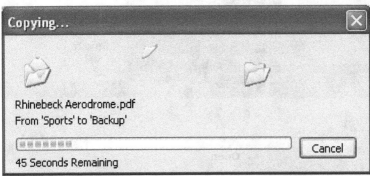

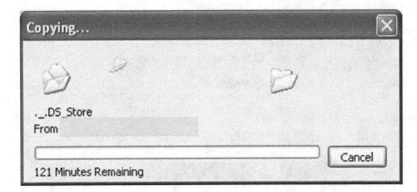

You get the screen that tells you the target (backup) folder already contains a file with this name (well Duh...this is a backup folder) and asks you if you would like to replace it? Then it gives you the details (date and time the file was modified) and the option to do this for all or just this one.

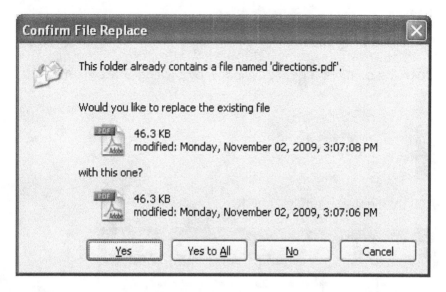

Given these limited choices, to make sure you backup all the latest updates you would need to select "Yes To All" and then wait the 121 minutes while this overwrites all the files. This is not a good idea because:

It wastes your time and slows down your computer.

Every time you overwrite something you risk corrupting the file.

So logically what you want to do if you could be in control is to only overwrite the files which are newer on the source drive than they are on the backup, and copy over any files from the source that do not currently exist on the backup.

Sounds pretty simple and logical, but how do you do this?

The answer lies hidden in the old DOS commands.

Back in the old days of DOS, this was a very routine task for us old time computer geeks. But now in the days of graphical interfaces and flashy apps, this is not as apparent. Windows will show you what's inside a folder, but the screen only shows you 50 or so files and then you need to scroll down. If you want to make a text file or spreadsheet listing the file names, you cannot copy and paste these.

So here is what you do.

Open the command prompt Window by clicking **Start->Run**

And then enter "cmd", click "OK"

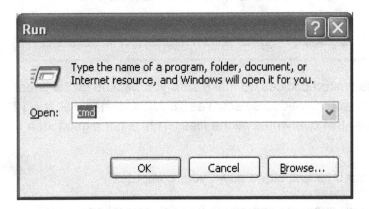

Change the default directory (the old name for Folder) to be what you are looking for by typing "**cd /D X:\Folder\SubFolder**", where "X" is the drive letter and Folder is the first level folder and SubFolder is the next, etc until you have the complete path to the files you are looking for.

In this example – "cd /D C:\Documents and Settings\koppe\My Documents\Sports"

You can paste this comment into a text or WORD file and then copy and paste it into the Command window using the Edit function –

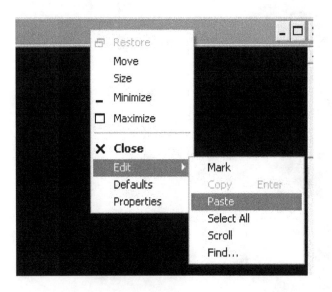

```
C:\ C:\WINDOWS\system32\cmd.exe
Microsoft Windows XP [Version 5.1.2600]
(C) Copyright 1985-2001 Microsoft Corp.

H:\>cd /D C:\Documents and Settings\koppe\My Documents\Sports
```

Then press "Enter".

```
C:\ C:\WINDOWS\system32\cmd.exe
Microsoft Windows XP [Version 5.1.2600]
(C) Copyright 1985-2001 Microsoft Corp.

H:\>cd /D C:\Documents and Settings\koppe\My Documents\Sports

C:\Documents and Settings\koppe\My Documents\Sports>
```

The prompt that comes before the ">" tells you the folder (we used to call them "directory") you are now in.

If you want to see all the files in that folder (to be sure you are in the right place), you can type "dir" and press "enter".

```
C:\WINDOWS\system32\cmd.exe                                          - □ ×
Microsoft Windows XP [Version 5.1.2600]
(C) Copyright 1985-2001 Microsoft Corp.

H:\>cd /D C:\Documents and Settings\koppe\My Documents\Sports

C:\Documents and Settings\koppe\My Documents\Sports>dir
 Volume in drive C is OSDisk
 Volume Serial Number is 4288-7BD7

 Directory of C:\Documents and Settings\koppe\My Documents\Sports

04/15/2013  02:27 PM    <DIR>          .
04/15/2013  02:27 PM    <DIR>          ..
11/10/2008  05:26 PM            36,864 2008 Wreath Sale Order Sheet.doc
12/05/2012  11:12 AM            56,320 Basketball Princeton 2013.xls
12/04/2012  03:51 PM            15,825 Basketball Schedule.R2.TEST.xlsx
12/05/2012  11:07 AM            43,008 Basketball Schedule.R2.xls
12/04/2012  04:00 PM            15,814 Basketball Schedule.R2.xlsx
12/07/2010  10:47 AM            23,922 boy scout knots 2.pdf
10/25/2012  11:09 AM           347,463 BSA Med 2012.E.Kopp.pdf
11/02/2009  03:07 PM            47,424 directions.pdf
04/20/2009  08:40 AM            62,464 Egypt Speech.doc
04/15/2013  02:27 PM    <DIR>          Fill In Forms
03/05/2013  11:34 AM            13,222 Letter of Recommendations Guideline.doc
03/13/2008  08:40 AM           128,000 Map to Kittatinny Mountain Scout Reservation.doc
12/10/2012  03:27 PM            89,088 MBA_Rec_Rules_and_Regs_20131 docm.doc
02/15/2013  02:10 PM            20,740 MeritBadgeCounselorApproval.FEB2013.pdf
02/28/2012  05:45 PM           330,111 New Med Form parts_ab.pdf
02/28/2012  05:46 PM           400,975 New Med Form part_c.pdf
02/28/2012  05:46 PM           263,694 New Med Form part_d.pdf
01/09/2009  03:24 PM           192,730 Reading.pdf
10/07/2009  02:47 PM           865,425 Rhinebeck Aerodrome.pdf
06/10/2008  04:03 PM            25,846 s05_important_prep_memo.pdf
06/10/2008  04:02 PM            16,416 s08_summer_camp_gear_list.pdf
02/13/2013  01:04 PM           182,549 s16_scout_uniform_guide.pdf
01/05/2009  04:26 PM         1,014,082 s20_semeos_merit_badge_program_rules_2009.pdf
02/06/2012  05:46 PM            12,229 ScoutTraxAdvance (2).pdf
01/08/2009  05:18 PM            66,515 Star Spangled Banner-Score[1].pdf
01/08/2009  05:18 PM            17,748 StarSpangledBanner-Voice[1].pdf
05/06/2010  09:34 AM            51,189 Strawberry Fest Sponsor Letter.pdf
04/16/2009  09:11 AM           296,467 Strawberry Festival 2009.pdf
03/11/2013  08:03 AM            76,343 Troop Full Roster By Patrols Mar 2013.pdf
01/08/2009  05:24 PM           273,375 USAAnthem[1].pdf
11/02/2009  03:03 PM            73,903 visit.pdf
05/07/2008  12:53 PM           329,216 Yards Creek Scout Reservation.doc
05/07/2008  12:53 PM           312,251 Yards Creek Scout Reservation.pdf
              32 File(s)      5,701,218 bytes
               3 Dir(s)  197,673,779,200 bytes free

C:\Documents and Settings\koppe\My Documents\Sports>
```

Now you need to copy only the new files over to you backup drive/folder.

To do this without overwriting everything like in Windows, use a command called "XCOPY". XCOPY lets you have a lot of control over what is copied and what is not.

The format for this command is: XCOPY source destination /switch

A switch is an instruction added onto command to tell it to do specific things.

For this purpose of making an incremental backup (copying only those things which have changed since the last backup), you would use this format for the command:

xcopy *.* F:\Backup /D/S/C/F/R/Y

To break this down –

xcopy is the command which can copy all files, folders and subfolders and keep everything in order as it found it.

. tells xcopy to copy everything in the current folder (all files, folders, subfolders, and all files in those folders and subfolders)

F:\Backup tells xcopy to place all the copied files and folders in F:\Backup (a folder on a USB zip drive in this example).

/D tells xcopy to copy files whose time stamp on the source folder is newer than in the destination folder (i.e. they have been modified since the last time they were copied).

/S tells xcopy to copy all folders and subfolders unless they are empty (contain no files).

/C tells xcopy to continue copying even if errors occur (you do not want to be bothered while this is working – not all errors are critical – better to review them later when this is done).

/F tells xcopy to displays the full source and destination file names while copying (this is a personal preference - it shows the full paths of the files it is copying, just to make sure we are finding the right ones).

/R tells xcopy to overwrite read-only files (you need to back up ALL files).

/Y tells xcopy to suppress prompting to you to confirm you want to overwrite an existing backup file (you don't want to be bothered with this like Windows does. The /D command ensures you are only copying the files you need).

If you are always working with a fixed set of folders at the source and the destination, you can save this command in a text file and copy and paste it into the Command screen –

```
C:\WINDOWS\system32\cmd.exe
Microsoft Windows XP [Version 5.1.2600]
<C> Copyright 1985-2001 Microsoft Corp.

H:\>cd /D C:\Documents and Settings\koppe\My Documents\Sports

C:\Documents and Settings\koppe\My Documents\Sports>xcopy *.* F:\Backup /D/S/C/F/R/Y_
```

Then just click "Enter" -

```
C:\WINDOWS\system32\cmd.exe                                    _ □ ×
 -> F:\Backup\Fill In Forms\Strawberry Fest Sponsor Letter.pdf
C:\Documents and Settings\koppe\My Documents\Sports\Fill In Forms\Strawberry Festival 2009.pdf -> F:
\Backup\Fill In Forms\Strawberry Festival 2009.pdf
C:\Documents and Settings\koppe\My Documents\Sports\Fill In Forms\Troop Full Roster By Patrols Mar 2
013.pdf -> F:\Backup\Fill In Forms\Troop Full Roster By Patrols Mar 2013.pdf
C:\Documents and Settings\koppe\My Documents\Sports\Fill In Forms\USAAnthem[1].pdf -> F:\Backup\Fill
 In Forms\USAAnthem[1].pdf
C:\Documents and Settings\koppe\My Documents\Sports\Fill In Forms\visit.pdf -> F:\Backup\Fill In For
ms\visit.pdf
C:\Documents and Settings\koppe\My Documents\Sports\Fill In Forms\Yards Creek Scout Reservation.doc
-> F:\Backup\Fill In Forms\Yards Creek Scout Reservation.doc
C:\Documents and Settings\koppe\My Documents\Sports\Fill In Forms\Yards Creek Scout Reservation.pdf
-> F:\Backup\Fill In Forms\Yards Creek Scout Reservation.pdf
44 File(s) copied
```

And you have copied over 44 files in this example; only the ones that are newer than those in the "Backup" folder or the ones that did not exist in the "Backup" folder.

If you keep these commands handy in a text file, you can copy and paste them as you need them. This will run in the background and use much less processor capacity than Windows copy, so you will not notice any significant slowdown of your computer.

Try it – a few minutes invested every day can save weeks or months of hard work recreating these files if the network goes down or even if you accidentally overwrite the primary file. Don't count on the "Network Guys" to bail you out.